Larry Walker

CANADIAN ROCKY

by
Tony DeMarco

SPORTS PUBLISHING INC.
www.SportsPublishingInc.com

©1999 Sports Publishing Inc.

Production manager: Susan M. McKinney
Cover design: Scot Muncaster
Photos: *The Associated Press*, Mr. and Mrs. Larry Walker Sr., Maple Ridge
Secondary School; Rich Clarkson and Associates

ISBN: 1-58261-052-5
Library of Congress Catalog Card Number: 99-61955

SPORTS PUBLISHING INC.
SportsPublishingInc.com

Printed in the United States.

CONTENTS

As a teenager, Larry (30) dreamed of being a goalie in the National Hockey League. (Photos courtesy of Mr. and Mrs. Larry Walker Sr.)

CHAPTER ONE

The End of a Dream

The ride was a long, lonely one. Through the Canadian province of Saskatchewan, Larry Walker, then an aspiring 16-year-old hockey goalie, sat in the passenger seat of a car with the father of his friend, Rick Herbert.

The two were on their way from Regina to Swift Current, a small town of 15,000 people about 1,000 miles from Larry's home in Maple Ridge, British Columbia. This wasn't exactly what Larry had in mind when it came to pursuing his dream to play in the National Hockey League, but at this point, he had no other choice.

Colorado Avalanche goalie Patrick Roy is Larry's favorite athlete. (AP/Wide World Photos)

Like almost all teenage boys growing up in Canada, Larry's favorite sport wasn't baseball, but hockey. In fact, many years later, after he had spent a decade as a star major-league baseball player, Larry said he still wished he was a hockey player, and that his favorite pro athlete is Patrick Roy, the goalie for the Colorado Avalanche.

Goalie was always Larry's position, just as it was for one of his three older brothers, Carey. Larry tagged along with his father to watch Carey play in the amateur Junior A Hockey League. Carey was good enough to be drafted by the Montreal Canadians, but never made it in the NHL.

Larry climbed through the ranks of organized youth hockey in British Columbia with Herbert and another friend, Cam Neely, who went on to score 395 goals in a 13-year career in the NHL. The three played as often as they could together, usually with Herbert and Neely going one-on-one and trying to score on Larry.

One of Larry's childhood friends was former NHL star Cam Neely. (AP/Wide World Photos)

Their careers flourished to the point that Larry and Herbert attended a tryout camp for the Regina Pats of the Junior A Hockey League. Junior A hockey was the goal for Canadian teenage players. The teams are located in the bigger cities and play at first-rate rinks. Pro scouts attend almost every game, looking for prospects, so it usually is a stepping stone to a professional contract.

Herbert made the Pats as a defenseman, but Larry played in only one practice game before he was offered a chance to be the starting goalie for the Pats' Tier Two farm team in Swift Current, one level below the Pats. Herbert's dad agreed to drive a disappointed Larry to Swift Current, but when they arrived in the small town, Larry knew it wasn't for him.

"It was a tough place, kind of dirty," Larry said later. "I said to myself, 'what am I doing here?' Then we went to the rink, and when I got there, I told myself, 'No, I didn't want to do it.' It just wasn't what I wanted. We hopped back in the car and drove home."

A week or so later, there was another opportunity but the end result was the same. Larry tried out for the Junior A team in Kelowna, a ski resort town in British Columbia. Once again, he quickly was assigned to a Tier Two farm team.

Tired of being promised things that didn't materialize, Larry again declined the offer, went back home to Maple Ridge and gave up on a dream with no idea that a brilliant career in another professional sport was in his future.

2

Playing a New Game

Until he was 16, Larry played very little baseball. The short summers in British Columbia limited baseball seasons in the youth leagues around Maple Ridge to less than 20 games. There also was no baseball team at Larry's high school.

Having decided to put hockey behind him, Larry turned his attention to baseball. After a successful summer with the Coquitlam Reds, a traveling team for 16 and 17-year-olds that played around British Columbia, he was selected to attend a try-

High school sophomore Larry Walker. (Maple Ridge Secondary School)

out camp for a team that would represent Canada in the 1984 World Youth Championships in Kindersley, Saskatchewan.

This time, there was a spot on the team for Larry, and during the tournament, he impressed Montreal Expos' scouting director Jim Fanning enough that the team offered him a contract a few months later.

Because of his inexperience and very raw skills —after all, Larry played only 15 to 20 games each summer—Larry was offered only $1,500 to sign. He said later he would have signed for nothing.

"They said, 'Here's what we're going to give you.' I said, 'Thanks,'" Larry said. "I had no idea what I was getting into. I was just going to go and have fun, as far as I was concerned."

Larry struggled in his first pro season at Utica, New York, as his inexperience showed in a league in which most of the players had collegiate experience. Larry batted only .223 with two home runs and 26 RBI in 215 at-bats. But there were enough signs of good things to come, and so much improvement from the beginning of the season, that the Expos knew they had a major-league prospect on their hands.

During the 1986 season, Larry moved from first base and third base to the outfield, where his speed and strong arm were better utilized. He started to blossom offensively as well, as he hit .289 with 29 home runs and 74 RBI in 332 at-bats and 95 games for Class A Burlington, Iowa.

Before that season ended, he was promoted again to the Expos' farm team in West Palm Beach, Florida, and finished with a .283 batting average, four homers and 16 RBI in 113 at-bats.

Throughout his rapid progress, Larry never stopped trying to get better.

"I was smart enough to listen to my coaches, and I worked hard in practice," Larry said. "I knew very little. I had everything to gain. I had a lot to learn, but I ate it all up.

"One thing I've always been able to do is rise to whatever level I'm playing in. If I saw somebody who was better than me, I would watch them, and try to find a way to get up to that level."

There was another step up for Larry in 1987 to Double A Jacksonville, Florida. He continued to excel despite being just 20 years old, and hit .287 with 26 homers and 83 RBI in 474 at-bats that season. He was named to the Southern League All-Star team.

There also was his first major honor, as Larry received the James "Tip" O'Neill Award as the top baseball player in Canada. The trophy is named after the Canadian-born outfielder who played in the majors and is a member of the Canadian Baseball Hall of Fame.

Just when it appeared as if nothing would slow Larry's progress to the majors, he suffered a major knee injury while playing winter baseball in Hermosillo, Mexico. Scoring from second base on a single, Larry slipped on home plate. His right knee locked up, and his body flipped over in an ugly somersault.

The injury occurred just one month before Larry would have reported to his first major-league spring-training camp with the Expos. Instead, he had to undergo major reconstructive surgery to repair damage in all three main cartilages in his knee. He had to spend eight weeks in a cast and then endured a grueling seven-month rehabilitation program.

To this day, Larry still hasn't regained all the strength in his right knee, which is slightly smaller than his left one.

He didn't play at all during the 1988 season, and calls the injury the low point of his career.

"I thought to myself, 'I'm done,'" he said. "My career might be over. It was a big setback to overcome."

Healthy enough to resume his career, Larry was assigned to Triple A Indianapolis for the start of the 1989 season.

Slowly, he regained his strength and skills, and by August 16, he was hitting .270 with 12 home runs, 59 RBI and 36 stolen bases—the most of his career. Not only was he able to overcome his injury, he was on his way to the major leagues.

Larry made his first major league appearance on August 16, 1989. (Montreal Expos)

Native Son

Only 20 months removed from major reconstructive knee surgery that threatened his career, Larry made his major-league debut against the San Francisco Giants on August 16, 1989.

He walked in his first two at-bats, and then singled to left field in his first official at-bat. He was the fifth Canadian native to wear an Expos uniform, and quickly developed into one of the best players in franchise history.

Larry was only the fifth Canadian to play for the Expos. (AP/Wide World Photos)

"At first, I just wanted to play baseball. It didn't matter what team I played for," Larry later said. "Eventually, playing in Montreal meant something. Just being a Canadian in the big leagues was a rarity, let alone to play with a Canadian team.

"I owe a lot to the Expos and the fans. The people were behind me there. I got a standing ovation on a double once. I try to remember the good times, and throw the other stuff out the window."

Larry got only eight hits in 47 at-bats over 20 games in the final weeks of the 1989 season, but he was in the majors to stay. He made the Expos roster out of spring training in 1990, and played regularly in his first full season, hitting .241 with 19 home runs, 51 RBI and 21 stolen bases.

That wasn't enough to be the best rookie on his team, as second baseman Delino DeShields finished second in the National League Rookie of the Year balloting to Atlanta's David Justice. Larry re-

Larry and Andres Galarraga, left, have been teammates in both Montreal and Colorado. (AP/Wide World Photos)

ceived only one third-place vote, even though his 19 homers tied Andre Dawson's club record for rookies.

By the second half of the 1991 season, Larry was beginning to show that he was one of the better players in the National League. He led all hitters with a .338 batting average after the All-Star break, had 10 homers and 41 RBIs in the second half, and was the Expos' player of the month in August when he batted .376.

Larry also had to move to first base after an injury to Andres Galarraga, and he played there during a perfect game thrown by Expos right-hander Dennis Martinez on July 28 at Los Angeles.

Larry's 1992 season—his third full season in the majors—was his best with the Expos. When it was over, he became the most-honored native Canadian baseball player in major-league history.

*Larry was Canada's Baseball Man of the Year in 1992.
(AP/Wide World Photos)*

Larry hit .301 with 23 home runs, 93 RBIs and 85 runs scored—all career highs at that point —stole 18 bases, led National League outfielders with 16 assists, and committed only two errors in right field. He was named to post-season All-Star teams by the Associated Press and *The Sporting News*. He received both a Silver Slugger award for offensive excellence and a Gold Glove award for defensive excellence. He was named the Expos' player of the year and for the first time was honored as Canada's Baseball Man of the Year. Larry even finished second to Olympic swimmer Mark Tewksbury as Canada's Male Athlete of the Year— not bad for a kid who wanted to be a hockey player.

"Larry is one of the most talented players in baseball," Expos general manager Kevin Malone said at the time. "He can beat you with his bat, his power, his glove, his arm and his speed. There's nothing the guy can't do.

"If he decided to hit for average and not for power, I think he could hit .330 or .340. And if he wanted to concentrate on power, I think he could hit 30 to 40 home runs. He's capable of doing anything he wants to do."

Larry also played in his first All-Star Game, and became the first Canadian to do so since George Selkirk represented the New York Yankees in 1939. In his only at-bat, Larry got a pinch-hit single off Juan Guzman of the Toronto Blue Jays.

The 1993 season brought Larry another Gold Glove award. Expos centerfielder Marquis Grissom also won one, making them only the third pair of outfield teammates ever to win the award in the same season.

Larry also became the first Canadian native to hit at least 20 homers and steal 20 bases in the same season. His batting average dipped to .265, however, and he missed 24 games because of injuries.

Meanwhile, the Expos continued to improve under popular manager Felipe Alou, who took over from Tom Runnells during the 1992 season. The team won the second-most games in franchise history, 94, but it wasn't enough to beat out the Philadelphia Phillies. Larry was disappointed by Montreal's second-place finish, but the real heartbreak was yet to come.

Larry signs autographs for fans at spring training in Arizona.
(AP/Wide World Photos)

Strike Out

The 1994 season would end on a bad note for Larry and the Expos, but it began with a humorous incident. In the third inning of a nationally televised game against the Dodgers on April 24, Mike Piazza hit a foul fly ball that Larry caught near the stands.

Mistakenly thinking it was the third out of the inning, Larry flipped the ball to a 9-year-old boy, Sebastian Napier, who was sitting in the first row. It was only the second out, and as soon as Larry realized it, he grabbed the ball back from the boy and threw it back into play.

The runner on first base, Jose Offerman, tagged up and advanced to third. At least the mistake turned out to be meaningless, as the next batter, Tim Wallach, hit a home run that cleared the bases.

"I gave the kid an autographed ball later, and I told him, 'don't ever take the ball out of my hand again,'" Larry said later.

Outside of his harmless goof, things were going quite well for Larry and the Expos. He was on his way to setting a career high with a .322 batting average, as well as leading the National League with 44 doubles. The Expos jumped into first place, as their powerful cast of players including Moises Alou, Marquis Grissom, Darrin Fletcher, Mike Lansing, Jeff Fassero, Pedro Martinez, John Wetteland, Ken Hill and Mel Rojas proved superior to the rest of the National League East.

By late-June, Larry's right shoulder was hurting. He had suffered a slight tear in his rotator cuff, and had to move from right field to first base. Despite the injury, he still was voted Expos player of the month in July, when he hit .355 with four homers and 24 RBIs.

The Expos remained in first place into August, and chances of the first World Series appearance in club history appeared quite good. But August 11 was the last day of baseball that season, as the Major League Baseball Players Association, upset that its demands weren't being met by owners, went on strike.

"We never thought the strike would go on as long as it did," Larry said. "It was really frustrating to have a team that good, and get nothing for it. We had the best record in baseball. That was our one and only chance to get to the World Series. I think we would have won the World Series. I really believe we would have."

Larry wouldn't play another game for the Expos. He was disgruntled with the Expos and their financial problems, and was eligible to become a free-agent by virtue of his six seasons in the major leagues. On the verge of winning a championship, the team was forced to trade three star players in addition to losing Larry, primarily because they couldn't afford to keep them.

In each case, the Expos took minor-league players in return, but nothing that would help them remain one of the best teams in the majors. While several teams expressed interest in signing Larry, the Expos made an offer that was nowhere near what was available elsewhere.

"The same thing has happened to every other player who's ever there and gotten some years under his belt," Larry said.

"You could make a pretty good all-star team from the guys the Expos have gotten rid of."

Where to go next wasn't really a very tough decision for Larry. When visiting Denver with the Expos, he was excited about the fan support the Colorado Rockies received. As a first-year expansion team in 1993, they set an all-time major-league record by drawing 4,483,350 fans.

The interest didn't wane in the second year, as an average of 58,598 fans attended each game at Mile High Stadium, and beginning in 1995, the Rockies would be moving into Coors Field. Turning down a couple of other four-year contract offers, Walker signed a four-year, $22.5-million deal on April 8, 1995. He would prove to be well worth the money.

"This was where I wanted to go," Larry said when he was introduced at a press conference at the club's spring-training headquarters in Tucson, Arizona.

Larry signed a four-year contract with the Rockies at the beginning of the 1995 season. He is sitting next to Rockies' owner Jerry McMorris. (AP/Wide World Photos)

"Fifty thousand people a game. That's six ballgames in Montreal. I think that was the biggest reason. I wanted to be with the Rockies. I'm going to do everything I can to make this a winning franchise, and I really think it can be."

Rockies fans had high expectations for Larry and the team in 1995. (AP/Wide World Photos)

On the Move

The 1995 season turned out even better than avid Rockies' fans could have hoped. In their first season, the Rockies finished in last place with a 67-95 record. In 1994 they improved to 53-64 before the strike prematurely ended the season.

With Larry, plus the addition of pitcher Bill Swift, who also was signed as a free agent, the Rockies' fans expected the team to be better in 1995.

Larry and Dante Bichette, left, were two-thirds of one of baseball's most powerful outfields in 1995. (AP/Wide World Photos)

Nobody was predicting an appearance in the playoffs, however. No expansion team in history had ever qualified for the postseason in such a short time.

From the beginning of the year, the Rockies proved they were a legitimate playoff contender. They christened Coors Field with a dramatic 11-9 victory in 14 innings over the New York Mets on Dante Bichette's game-winning home run. Fifteen games into the season, they were in first place in the National League West.

With Larry in the middle of the lineup surrounded by Bichette, Ellis Burks, Andres Galarraga and Vinny Castilla, the Rockies' offense was on a record-setting pace for runs, and quickly picked up the nickname "Blake Street Bombers" because Coors Field was located at the corner of Blake Street and 20th Avenue in downtown Denver. Larry, Bichette and Burks composed one of the most powerful outfields in baseball.

In 1995, Larry was one of the "Blake Street Bombers" in Denver. (AP/Wide World Photos)

"I just came from the best outfield in baseball with Marquis (Grissom) and Moises (Alou)," Larry said, "but now there might be a new best outfield in baseball, and it might be right here."

Larry led the way by hitting 36 homers for the season, second-most in the National League, by far the most in his career, and nine more than the record for most homers in a season by a Canadian native, previously set by Jeff Heath in 1947.

Five of those home runs came during a nine-game hitting streak in early May, and four of those came in consecutive games, which set a Rockies club record. One of those was the 100th of Larry's career.

Larry was the Rockies player of the month in June, when he batted .344 with eight homers and put together a 10-game hitting streak in which he batted .421. For the third season in a row, it wasn't good enough for Larry to make a return trip to the All-Star game.

Larry was disappointed when he was not selected for the
1995 All-Star team. (AP/Wide World Photos)

"I'm not one of the nine best outfielders in the league?" a disappointed Larry said. "That's kind of frustrating."

There would be a bigger prize at the end of the season. The Rockies won seven of eight to go into the All-Star break at 39-30, protecting a five-game lead in the division race. They stayed in first place alone until August 11, and never dropped more than 1½ games out of the top spot.

On the final day of the season, the Rockies needed a victory to make the playoffs, but found themselves trailing the Giants 8-2 in the third inning. Larry sparked the comeback with a double and a two-run home run, and the Rockies won 10-9 to cap an unexpectedly successful season.

The Rockies didn't get past the first round of the playoffs. They found themselves up against the powerful Atlanta Braves in the division series, and lost three of four games. While making the playoffs

In 1996, Larry moved from right field to center field. (AP/Wide World Photos)

was satisfying for Larry, it didn't make up for the disappointment of 1994.

"We had a great season, it came down to the last game and we had the big comeback to win it," Larry said. "That was huge. But that didn't make it easier as far as 1994. As a player, you want to win the World Series."

There would be a bigger disappointment in the 1996 season for Larry. Because he plays the game so hard, Larry has been prone to injuries throughout his career. The jinx struck again in 1996.

The season began with a position shift from right field to center field, a move manager Don Baylor wanted to make because he felt it improved the team's defense. Larry, one of the game's best right-fielders, reluctantly agreed.

"I'll do whatever is best for the team," Larry said.

In June 1996, Larry broke his collarbone on a play similar to this one and missed 60 games. (AP/Wide World Photos)

"I've won two Gold Gloves in right field, so it's a position I've played well. To switch to center, it's almost like I'm getting demoted. But if it's something they feel is right, let's go do it."

On June 9, Larry crashed into the wall in Coors Field while chasing a ball hit by Atlanta's Jeff Blauser and suffered a broken left collarbone. Larry missed a total of 60 games, and when he returned late in the season, he wasn't fully recovered.

Larry batted only .276 with 18 home runs, 58 RBI and 58 runs scored in 83 games in one of his worst seasons in the major leagues. The injury and disappointing performance only increased Larry's resolve to become a better player. Healed by the following spring, he was ready for the season that finally would elevate him to superstar status.

After his injury in 1996, Larry had a superstar season in 1997. (AP/Wide World Photos)

A Record-Setting Season

The feeling that 1997 would be a special season for Larry came very early in the year. On the very first weekend of the season, he and the Rockies were in Montreal for a four-game series, and on Saturday afternoon, Larry hit three home runs and drove in five runs in a 15-3 victory.

By the end of April, Larry was hitting an incredible .456 with 11 home runs and 29 RBIs. He was named the National League's Player of the Month. He kept his batting average above the cov-

After an intentionally wild pitch from Randy Johnson in the 1997 All-Star Game, Larry prompted laughter from the crowd by turning his batting helmet backwards. (AP/Wide World Photos)

eted .400 mark almost to the All-Star break, and was voted to the All-Star team as a starter.

Even before the game at Cleveland's Jacobs Field, Larry was a big hit, as he finished second in the home-run hitting contest to Tino Martinez of the New York Yankees. Larry hit the most home runs, and had the longest one in the contest at 479 feet, but he didn't hit as many as Martinez in the final round.

Larry drew a walk and made an out in his two at-bats during the game, but his hilarious confrontation with American League starting pitcher Randy Johnson in the second inning was one of the most off-beat moments in All-Star history.

Larry stepped into the left-hand batter's box, and Johnson's first pitch sailed six feet over his head —a pitch so obviously wild that it had to be a joke.

Larry then jumped across home plate into the right-hand batter's box, and flipped his batting helmet around backwards.

Johnson's next pitch also was a ball, and then Larry went back to batting from the left side, and drew a walk. Making the incident funny was the fact that one month earlier, Larry had sat out a game against Johnson, something almost all left-handed hitters do whenever the imposing 6'10" left-hander is pitching. But because Larry was hitting .409 at the time, it stirred up a controversy that remained an issue leading up to the All-Star game.

On the day before the game, Larry joked, "maybe I'll bat right-handed," but nobody took him seriously. Since Larry and Johnson were teammates in the Expos' minor-league system several years earlier, some people believe the two planned the incident, but if so, Larry wasn't saying afterward.

"I didn't even know if I was allowed to do that," Larry said. "I looked like Colonel Klink out there. I was laughing hysterically inside."

Now that Larry had everybody's attention, he showed over the rest of the season that he was much more than a jokester. His 493-foot home run into third deck on August 31 was the longest hit by a Rockies player at Coors Field. He hit five home runs the week of September 15-21, and was named National League Player of the Week.

When his truly historic season ended, he was only four hits and 10 RBI away from winning the National League Triple Crown. He finished first with 49 home runs, second with a .366 batting average and third with 130 RBI.

"Day after day, I was shocking myself at the things I did," Larry said. "The numbers went up, and the balls went out of the park. I'd go home at night, or back to the hotel, and say to myself, 'well, I did that again? I can't believe that. This is fun.'"

Larry's 409 total bases were the most in a season in almost 50 years. He also finished second in

The Rockies gave Larry a watch and a Harley Davidson motorcycle after he won the National League MVP Award in 1997. (AP/Wide World Photos)

runs scored with 143, and in hits with 208. Larry also won another Gold Glove, his third, and set a Rockies record by playing 128 consecutive games without an error.

"Larry put together a year they could not deny," Rockies manager Don Baylor said.

The Baseball Writers Association of America thought so, too. They made Larry a landslide winner in the National League Most Valuable Player Award balloting, as he received 22 of the 28 first-place votes, and finished with 359 points to beat Mike Piazza's 263. No other Canadian player has won the honor, and when it was time to talk about it, Larry went back to his roots.

"I love my parents to death," Larry said. "I called them as soon as I found out, and they started crying. But they can cry all they want. They're not getting (the MVP trophy).

Larry won the National League MVP award in 1997,
the only Canadian to ever earn such an honor.
(Colorado Rockies/Rich Clarkson and Associates)

"I'm from a very athletic family. I grew up with three older brothers who were all very competitive and good at what they did. I had a father who played sports and was good at what he did.

"I'm sure that has a lot to do with it. I've done something good for me personally, and even better, I've done something good for my country."

Larry has stolen 179 bases in his major-league career.
(AP/Wide World Photos)

Encore Performance

I t isn't easy following one of the great est seasons in baseball history, and making matters even worse for Larry as he prepared for the 1998 season was an injury that actually occurred at the end of his 1997 MVP campaign.

In the third-to-last game, he injured his right elbow when he swung at a pitch and missed. He sat out the final two games, missing a chance at hitting a 50th home run.

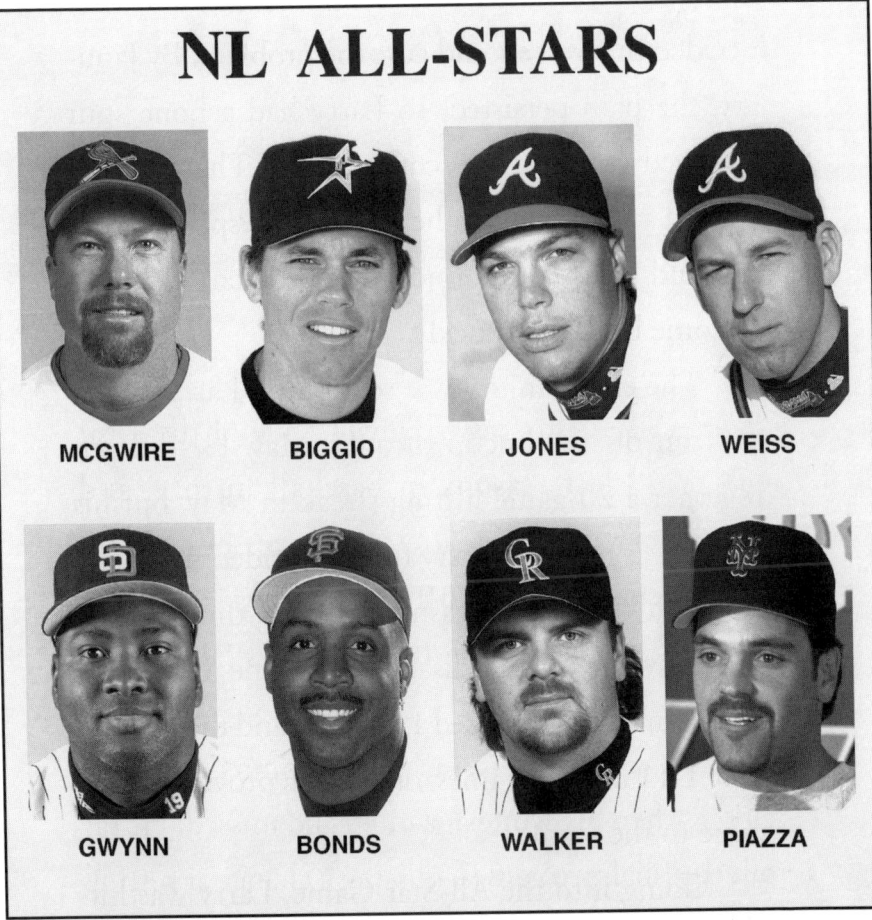

NL ALL-STARS

MCGWIRE   BIGGIO   JONES   WEISS

GWYNN   BONDS   WALKER   PIAZZA

Larry was a starter on the 1998 National League All-Star team. (AP/Wide World Photos)

Larry consulted with team doctors, and they decided that rest should cure the problem. By January, the pain persisted, so Larry had a bone spur removed during arthroscopic surgery. That put him behind schedule when he reported to spring training, and Larry compounded the problem by trying to come back too quickly.

The elbow injury was so painful, Larry was in and out of the lineup through May. He did put together a 20-game hitting streak in May, but his power was missing. Larry finally decided that playing with the injury wasn't the right thing to do, and he went on the disabled list June 19. Up to that point, he had missed 12 games, and the Rockies were 1-11 in those games, once again proving Larry's value to the team.

Going into the All-Star Game, Larry was hitting .331, but had only nine home runs and 33 RBIs. Despite the relatively low numbers, Larry was voted a starter for the National League team.

Larry batted .402 in the second half of the 1998 season. (AP/Wide World Photos)

Larry knew he was being rewarded more for what he had accomplished in 1997. "I don't deserve to start the game," Larry said. "I probably don't even deserve to be on the team. But the fans get their say, and I'm fortunate enough to be one of the three all-star outfielders."

What made the selection special was that the game was held in Coors Field. Larry walked in the third inning and eventually scored on Tony Gwynn's two-run single. He also popped out in his other at-bat.

The All-Star break also brought another big event for Larry, as he married Angela Brekken the day after the game. The wedding came one year after Larry proposed while the two were on a flight to the 1997 All-Star game.

The injury problems expanded after the All-Star break, but that didn't stop Larry from leading the league in hitting from that point, batting .402,

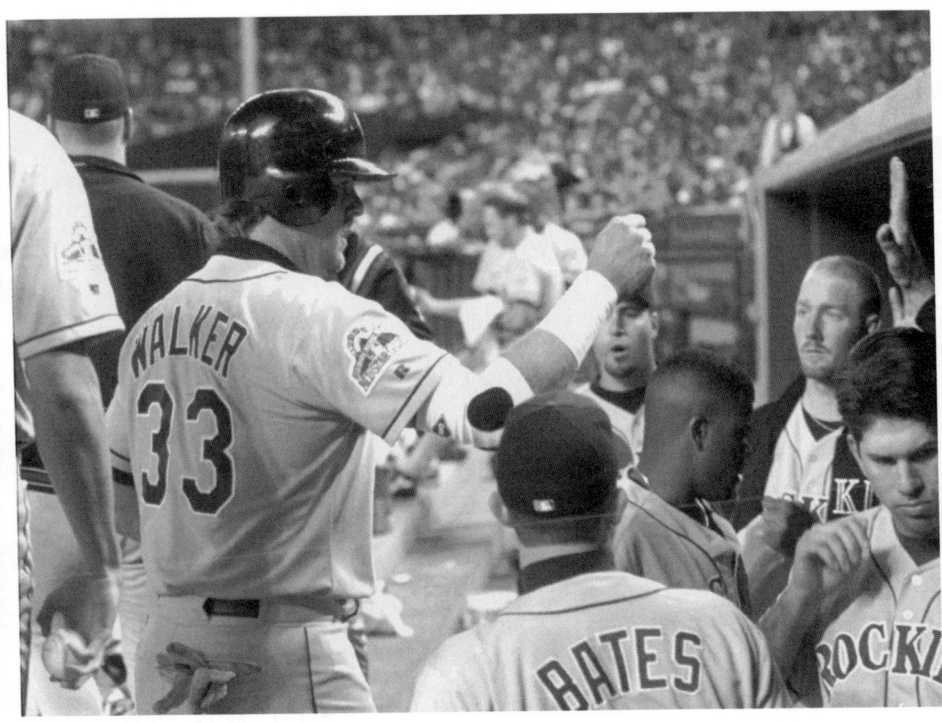

*Despite various injuries, Larry batted .363 in
1998 and won the National League batting title.
(AP/Wide World Photos)*

including a .528 mark in September. He missed eight games in August because of a sprained ligament in his right middle finger. He had taken over the league lead July 29, when he was hitting .340, and after the injury he came back and moved on top to stay on Sept. 4, when he raised his average to .344. Larry's average kept climbing from there, as he hit .531 over the final two weeks of the season and finished at .363, nine points ahead of John Olerud of the New York Mets.

With back-to-back seasons at .366 and .363, Larry raised his career batting average above the .300 mark for the first time to .305. His Coors Field batting average for the 1998 season was .418, but the batting title couldn't make up for Larry's disappointment with the Rockies' overall performance.

"It's a pleasant thing. I'm happy about it. But I'm not going out to celebrate it," Larry said about the batting title. "Our season is ending in Septem-

Larry, who has settled in the Denver area, poses with fans on a picture day in 1998. (AP/Wide World Photos)

ber. That's disappointing. Nothing could cheer me up more than winning the World Series."

Looking to 1999 and the future, both Larry and the Rockies want to continue their association. The two reached agreement on a contract extension that will keep Larry in place for another six seasons—possibly to the end of his career. That is fine with Larry, who has settled in the Denver area and plans to stay there even after he retires.

"This was where I wanted to come and play four years ago, and that hasn't changed," Larry said. "I still want to play here. It's a great place to play."

Larry watches the ball as he as he attempts to lay down a bunt. (AP/Wide World Photos)

Larry Walker Quick Facts

Full Name: Larry Kenneth Robert Walker
Team: Colorado Rockies
Hometown: Maple Ridge, British Columbia
Position: Outfielder
Jersey Number: 33
Bats: Left
Throws: Right
Height: 6-3 1/2
Weight: 220 pounds
Birthdate: December 1, 1966

1998 Highlight: Larry's league-leading .363 batting average in 1998 included a .418 average in 65 home games.

Stats Spotlight: During 19 games in September of 1998, Larry registered an amazing .528 average, collecting 28 hits in 53 at bats.

Little-Known Fact: Larry Walker is the first native Canadian to win a Most Valuable Player award in Major League Baseball.

Larry Walker's Major League Career

Year	Club	AVG	G	AB	R	H	2B	3B	HR	RBI	BB	SO	SB
1989	Montreal	.170	20	47	4	8	0	0	0	4	5	13	1
1990	Montreal	.241	133	419	59	101	18	3	19	51	49	112	21
1991	Montreal	.290	137	487	59	141	30	2	16	64	42	102	14
1992	Montreal	.301	143	528	85	159	31	4	23	93	41	97	18
1993	Montreal	.265	138	490	85	130	24	5	22	86	80	76	29
1994	Montreal	.322	103	395	76	127	44*	2	19	86	47	74	15
1995	Colorado	.306	131	494	96	151	31	5	36	101	49	72	16
1996	Colorado	.276	83	272	58	75	18	4	18	58	20	58	18
1997	Colorado	.366	153	568	143	208	46	4	49*	130	78	90	33
1998	Colorado	.363*	130	454	113	165	46	3	23	67	64	61	14
M.L. Totals		.305	1171	4154	778	1265	288	32	225	740	475	755	179

Active Career Batting Leaders

1.	Tony Gwynn	.339
2.	Mike Piazza	.333
3.	Wade Boggs	.329
4.	Frank Thomas	.321
5.	Edgar Martinez	.318
6.	Alex Rodriguez	.313
7.	Kenny Lofton	.311
8.	Rusty Greer	.310
9.	Mark Grace	.310
10.	Nomar Garciaparra	.309
15.	**Larry Walker**	**.305**

Active Career On Base Percentage Leaders

1.	Frank Thomas	.443
2.	Edgar Martinez	.424
3.	Wade Boggs	.416
4.	Jeff Bagwell	.411
5.	Barry Bonds	.411
6.	Jim Thome	.409
7.	Rickey Henderson	.404
8.	John Olerud	.403
9.	Mike Piazza	.396
10.	Tim Salmon	.395
24.	**Larry Walker**	**.382**

1998 National League Batting Average Leaders

Larry Walker	**.363**
John Olerud	.354
Dante Bichette	.331
Mike Piazza	.328
Jason Kendall	.327

1998 National League On-Base Percentage Leaders

Mark McGwire	.470
John Olerud	.447
Larry Walker	**.445**
Barry Bonds	.438
Gary Sheffield	.428

In 1998, Larry was third in the National League in slugging percentage, trailing only Mark McGwire and Sammy Sosa. (AP/Wide World Photos)

1998 National League Slugging Percentage Leaders

Mark McGwire	.752
Sammy Sosa	.647
Larry Walker	**.630**
Barry Bonds	.609
Greg Vaughn	.597

NL MVP Winners in the 1990s

1997	**Larry Walker, Colorado**
1996	Ken Caminiti, San Diego
1995	Barry Larkin, Cincinnati
1994	Jeff Bagwell, Houston
1993	Barry Bonds, San Francisco
1992	Barry Bonds, Pittsburgh
1991	Terry Pendleton, Atlanta
1990	Barry Bonds, Pittsburgh

Larry Walker's 1998 Game-by-Game Performance

Here's a game-by-game rundown of Larry Walker's 1998 season, a campaign in which he won the National League batting championship.

Date	Opp	AB	R	H	2B	3B	HR	RBI
3/31/98	@Ari	4	1	1	0	0	0	1
4/01/98	@Ari	3	3	2	2	0	0	1
4/02/98	@Ari	4	1	2	1	0	0	0
4/03/98	@Hou	3	0	0	0	0	0	0
4/04/98	@Hou	2	1	1	1	0	0	0
4/05/98	@Hou	4	0	0	0	0	0	0
4/07/98	StL	5	1	3	1	0	0	0
4/08/98	StL	5	0	1	0	0	0	1
4/09/98	StL	4	1	1	1	0	0	1
4/12/98	CIN	5	1	2	1	0	0	0

Date	Opp	AB	R	H	2B	3B	HR	RBI
4/13/98	CIN	4	1	1	1	0	0	0
4/14/98	LA	4	1	2	0	0	0	1
4/16/98	LA	4	1	1	0	0	0	0
4/18/98	ATL	4	2	2	1	0	0	0
4/19/98	ATL	3	1	3	0	0	0	0
4/19/98	ATL	4	3	3	0	0	1	1
4/20/98	ATL	4	0	1	0	0	0	0
4/22/98	@Fla	3	0	0	0	0	0	0
4/23/98	@Fla	2	1	0	0	0	0	0
4/24/98	@Fla	4	0	2	0	0	0	0
4/25/98	@Atl	4	1	2	0	1	0	2
4/26/98	@Atl	4	1	1	1	0	0	0
4/27/98	FLA	2	1	1	0	0	0	1
4/28/98	FLA	3	0	0	0	0	0	0
4/30/98	@NYN	3	0	1	0	0	0	0

Date	Opp	AB	R	H	2B	3B	HR	RBI
5/02/98	@NYN	2	1	1	0	0	1	1
5/03/98	@NYN	4	0	0	0	0	0	0
5/04/98	@Phi	3	1	1	1	0	0	0
5/05/98	@Phi	5	2	1	0	0	1	1
5/06/98	@Phi	2	1	1	0	0	1	4
5/07/98	@Mon	4	0	1	0	0	0	1
5/08/98	@Mon	5	1	1	1	0	0	0
5/10/98	@Mon	3	1	1	1	0	0	0
5/11/98	@Pit	4	1	2	0	0	0	0
5/12/98	@Pit	4	0	1	0	0	0	0
5/13/98	ChN	2	0	1	0	0	0	0
5/14/98	ChN	6	2	3	2	0	0	1
5/15/98	MIL	4	1	1	1	0	0	0
5/16/98	MIL	5	1	2	1	0	0	0
5/17/98	MIL	3	0	1	1	0	0	0

Date	Opp	AB	R	H	2B	3B	HR	RBI
5/18/98	MIL	5	0	2	2	0	0	0
5/20/98	@Atl	4	1	1	0	0	1	1
5/21/98	@Atl	3	0	1	0	0	0	0
5/22/98	@Cin	5	1	2	0	0	0	1
5/23/98	@Cin	3	1	1	0	0	0	0
5/24/98	@Cin	4	1	2	2	0	0	0
5/25/98	@StL	5	1	1	1	0	0	1
5/27/98	@StL	4	0	0	0	0	0	0
5/28/98	@StL	4	0	1	0	0	0	0
5/29/98	HOU	3	1	1	0	0	1	5
5/30/98	HOU	4	1	1	0	0	1	2
5/31/98	HOU	4	1	1	0	0	0	1
6/01/98	ARI	4	1	1	1	0	0	0
6/02/98	ARI	4	1	1	1	0	0	0
6/03/98	ARI	4	2	2	1	0	0	0

Date	Opp	AB	R	H	2B	3B	HR	RBI
6/04/98	ARI	4	0	2	1	0	0	1
6/05/98	@Ana	2	0	0	0	0	0	0
6/06/98	@Ana	4	0	0	0	0	0	0
6/07/98	@Ana	0	0	0	0	0	0	0
6/10/98	TEX	1	0	0	0	0	0	0
6/12/98	@LA	4	0	2	0	0	0	1
6/13/98	@LA	3	2	3	1	0	1	2
6/14/98	@LA	4	1	1	0	0	1	1
6/15/98	@SF	3	1	1	1	0	0	0
6/16/98	@SF	2	1	1	0	0	0	0
6/17/98	@SF	1	0	0	0	0	0	0
7/03/98	@SD	3	1	0	0	0	0	0
7/04/98	@SD	4	0	2	1	0	0	0
7/05/98	@SD	3	0	0	0	0	0	0
7/10/98	SF	4	0	0	0	0	0	0

Date	Opp	AB	R	H	2B	3B	HR	RBI
7/11/98	SF	4	0	0	0	0	0	0
7/12/98	SF	3	0	1	1	0	0	0
7/13/98	SD	5	2	2	1	0	1	1
7/14/98	SD	5	1	1	0	0	0	0
7/15/98	SD	3	1	1	0	0	0	1
7/17/98	@Ari	4	0	0	0	0	0	0
7/18/98	@Ari	4	0	1	0	0	0	0
7/19/98	@Ari	4	0	2	0	0	0	0
7/20/98	@Hou	5	3	3	1	0	0	1
7/21/98	@Hou	2	1	0	0	0	0	0
7/23/98	CIN	3	1	3	0	0	0	0
7/23/98	CIN	3	2	2	0	0	1	2
7/24/98	StL	3	1	2	0	2	0	2
7/25/98	StL	4	1	2	1	0	0	1
7/26/98	StL	4	0	1	1	0	0	0

Date	Opp	AB	R	H	2B	3B	HR	RBI
7/27/98	PIT	5	2	2	1	0	1	1
7/28/98	PIT	5	3	3	0	0	2	3
7/31/98	@ChN	1	0	1	0	0	0	1
8/01/98	@ChN	5	0	4	1	0	0	0
8/02/98	@ChN	5	0	1	0	0	0	1
8/03/98	@Pit	5	0	1	0	0	0	0
8/04/98	@Pit	4	1	0	0	0	0	0
8/05/98	@Pit	4	1	1	0	0	0	0
8/07/98	NYN	4	2	2	0	0	1	2
8/08/98	NYN	5	0	2	0	0	0	1
8/09/98	NYN	4	1	1	1	0	0	0
8/10/98	MON	3	2	1	0	0	1	1
8/11/98	MON	4	2	2	0	0	0	0
8/12/98	MON	3	1	0	0	0	0	0
8/14/98	PHI	4	0	2	1	0	0	0

Date	Opp	AB	R	H	2B	3B	HR	RBI
8/15/98	PHI	5	1	2	0	0	0	0
8/16/98	PHI	5	1	1	0	0	1	1
8/18/98	@NYN	5	1	1	1	0	0	1
8/18/98	@NYN	2	1	0	0	0	0	0
8/23/98	@Phi	0	0	0	0	0	0	0
8/24/98	@Phi	0	0	0	0	0	0	0
8/26/98	MIL	1	0	0	0	0	0	0
8/27/98	ChN	5	3	3	1	0	0	1
8/28/98	ChN	4	2	2	1	0	1	2
8/29/98	ChN	4	2	2	0	0	1	1
8/30/98	ChN	4	1	1	0	0	1	1
9/01/98	@Mil	3	2	2	1	0	0	1
9/02/98	@Mil	4	0	0	0	0	0	0
9/03/98	@Mil	3	1	2	0	0	0	0
9/04/98	SD	1	3	1	0	0	0	1

Date	Opp	AB	R	H	2B	3B	HR	RBI
9/05/98	SD	2	0	1	0	0	0	0
9/06/98	SD	3	2	3	0	0	0	1
9/07/98	FLA	4	3	3	0	0	2	2
9/08/98	FLA	2	1	1	0	0	0	0
9/09/98	FLA	4	1	2	0	0	0	1
9/11/98	@SF	2	1	1	0	0	0	0
9/12/98	@SF	4	1	2	1	0	0	0
9/13/98	@SF	4	0	1	0	0	0	0
9/18/98	@SD	3	0	0	0	0	0	0
9/20/98	@SD	1	1	1	1	0	0	0
9/22/98	ARI	1	0	0	0	0	0	0
9/23/98	ARI	3	0	3	0	0	0	1
9/25/98	SF	1	0	0	0	0	0	0
9/26/98	SF	4	3	3	1	0	1	1
9/27/98	SF	4	2	2	0	0	0	1
Totals		454	113	165	46	3	23	67

AVERAGE: .363

Larry Walker's 1997
Game-by-Game Performance

Date	Opp	AB	R	H	2B	3B	HR	RBI
4/01/97	@Cin	4	0	0	0	0	0	0
4/02/97	@Cin	3	1	1	0	0	1	1
4/03/97	@Cin	5	2	3	1	0	1	3
4/04/97	@Mon	4	2	2	1	0	1	2
4/05/97	@Mon	5	3	4	0	0	3	5
4/06/97	@Mon	4	0	1	0	0	0	0
4/07/97	CIN	4	1	2	1	1	0	2
4/09/97	CIN	5	2	3	0	0	0	0
4/12/97	MON	2	3	1	0	0	1	2
4/13/97	MON	2	0	0	0	0	0	0
4/14/97	MON	4	3	3	1	0	0	3
4/15/97	@ChN	4	2	4	0	0	2	4
4/16/97	@ChN	3	0	0	0	0	0	0
4/18/97	ATL	4	0	1	0	0	0	0
4/19/97	ATL	4	1	1	1	0	0	0

4/20/97	ATL	5	2	4	1	0	0	1
4/22/97	FLA	5	1	4	0	0	0	2
4/23/97	FLA	3	0	0	0	0	0	0
4/25/97	@StL	3	2	1	0	0	1	1
4/26/97	@StL	4	1	1	0	0	0	0
4/27/97	@StL	4	0	2	0	0	0	0
4/28/97	@Hou	5	1	1	0	0	0	0
4/30/97	ChN	4	2	2	0	0	1	3
5/01/97	ChN	3	0	0	0	0	0	0
5/02/97	PHI	4	2	1	0	0	0	0
5/03/97	PHI	5	0	0	0	0	0	0
5/04/97	PHI	5	2	3	2	0	0	4
5/05/97	NYN	4	0	1	0	0	0	0
5/06/97	NYN	4	2	2	1	0	0	1
5/07/97	PIT	4	0	2	0	0	0	0
5/08/97	PIT	4	1	1	0	0	1	2
5/09/97	@Phi	2	1	1	0	0	1	1
5/10/97	@Phi	3	0	0	0	0	0	0
5/11/97	@Phi	4	0	1	1	0	0	0
5/12/97	@Phi	4	2	2	1	0	0	2

5/14/97 @Pit	5	1	2	0	0	0	1
5/15/97 @Pit	4	1	2	1	0	0	1
5/16/97 @NYN	3	1	2	0	0	1	2
5/17/97 @NYN	4	0	1	0	0	0	0
5/18/97 @NYN	4	0	2	1	0	0	0
5/19/97 @NYN	0	0	0	0	0	0	0
5/20/97 @SF	4	1	2	1	0	0	0
5/21/97 @SF	5	0	1	0	0	0	1
5/22/97 @SF	4	0	1	0	0	0	0
5/23/97 HOU	3	2	2	1	0	0	0
5/24/97 HOU	2	0	1	1	0	0	0
5/25/97 HOU	4	0	1	0	1	0	1
5/26/97 StL	4	1	1	1	0	0	0
5/27/97 StL	4	0	3	0	1	0	1
5/29/97 @Fla	2	1	2	0	0	1	1
5/30/97 @Fla	3	1	0	0	0	0	0
5/31/97 @Fla	3	3	1	0	0	0	0
6/02/97 @StL	3	2	2	0	0	0	1
6/03/97 @StL	2	0	0	0	0	0	0
6/04/97 SD	5	2	2	1	0	0	0

Date	Team							
6/05/97	SD	5	3	3	1	0	2	3
6/07/97	FLA	4	1	2	0	0	1	1
6/08/97	FLA	3	2	2	1	0	0	0
6/08/97	FLA	3	0	1	0	0	0	0
6/09/97	ATL	4	0	3	0	0	0	1
6/10/97	ATL	3	0	0	0	0	0	0
6/11/97	ATL	3	0	0	0	0	0	0
6/12/97	@Sea	6	0	2	0	0	0	1
6/14/97	@Oak	3	3	2	1	0	1	1
6/15/97	@Oak	4	1	3	0	0	1	1
6/17/97	TEX	5	1	1	1	0	0	1
6/18/97	TEX	5	2	3	1	0	0	1
6/19/97	@SD	5	0	2	1	0	0	3
6/20/97	@SD	3	1	1	0	0	0	0
6/21/97	@SD	5	2	2	0	0	1	1
6/22/97	@SD	0	0	0	0	0	0	0
6/23/97	@LA	3	0	0	0	0	0	0
6/24/97	@LA	2	2	1	0	0	1	2
6/25/97	@LA	4	0	1	1	0	0	0
6/26/97	SF	3	0	1	0	0	0	0

6/27/97 SF	4	0	1	0	0	0	0
6/28/97 SF	4	3	2	0	0	1	1
6/29/97 SF	3	1	2	0	0	1	2
6/30/97 ANA	4	2	1	0	0	1	1
7/01/97 ANA	4	0	0	0	0	0	0
7/02/97 @Tex	4	0	0	0	0	0	0
7/04/97 @SF	3	0	0	0	0	0	0
7/05/97 @SF	3	0	2	0	0	0	0
7/06/97 @SF	3	0	2	0	0	0	0
7/10/97 SD	3	2	2	0	0	1	3
7/11/97 SD	4	1	1	0	0	0	0
7/12/97 SD	5	1	3	2	0	0	1
7/13/97 SD	4	1	3	1	0	0	4
7/14/97 LA	6	3	4	0	0	0	2
7/15/97 LA	4	0	0	0	0	0	0
7/16/97 @Atl	4	0	1	0	0	0	0
7/17/97 @Atl	4	1	1	0	0	1	1

7/19/97 @ChN	4	0	0	0	0	0	0
7/19/97 @ChN	5	0	0	0	0	0	0
7/20/97 @ChN	5	2	3	0	0	2	4
7/21/97 @Mon	2	0	0	0	0	0	0
7/22/97 @Mon	1	0	0	0	0	0	0
7/24/97 ChN	3	3	2	2	0	0	1
7/25/97 ChN	3	1	1	0	0	0	1
7/26/97 ChN	3	1	0	0	0	0	0
7/27/97 ChN	4	0	0	0	0	0	0
7/28/97 MON	3	0	0	0	0	0	0
7/29/97 MON	4	0	1	0	0	0	0
7/30/97 MON	4	1	2	1	0	0	2
7/31/97 @Pit	3	1	1	0	0	1	1
8/01/97 @Pit	5	3	3	1	0	2	2
8/02/97 @Pit	4	2	3	1	0	1	2

8/03/97 @Pit	4	1	3	1	0	0	1
8/04/97 @Phi	3	1	0	0	0	0	0
8/05/97 @Phi	5	0	0	0	0	0	0
8/06/97 @NYN	5	0	2	0	0	0	0
8/08/97 PIT	4	0	2	0	0	0	1
8/09/97 PIT	5	2	3	1	0	2	3
8/10/97 PIT	5	0	0	0	0	0	0
8/12/97 PHI	4	0	0	0	0	0	0
8/13/97 PHI	4	0	0	0	0	0	0
8/15/97 NYN	4	1	1	0	0	1	2
8/16/97 NYN	3	2	3	1	1	0	1
8/17/97 NYN	3	1	1	0	0	0	1
8/19/97 @Cin	5	0	0	0	0	0	0
8/20/97 @Cin	3	0	0	0	0	0	0
8/21/97 @Hou	4	1	2	0	0	0	1
8/22/97 @Hou	2	0	0	0	0	0	0

8/23/97 @Hou	0	1	0	0	0	0	0
8/25/97 CIN	4	1	2	0	0	1	1
8/25/97 CIN	5	1	3	2	0	0	0
8/26/97 CIN	4	0	1	0	0	0	0
8/27/97 CIN	3	2	1	1	0	0	0
8/28/97 SEA	5	0	1	0	0	0	1
8/29/97 SEA	4	1	2	1	0	1	1
8/30/97 OAK	4	2	2	1	0	0	0
8/31/97 OAK	4	2	3	0	0	2	4
9/01/97 @Ana	4	0	1	0	0	0	1
9/02/97 @Ana	3	2	1	0	0	1	1
9/05/97 StL	5	3	1	1	0	0	0
9/06/97 StL	6	2	3	0	0	1	2
9/06/97 StL	2	0	0	0	0	0	0
9/07/97 StL	0	1	0	0	0	0	0
9/09/97 HOU	4	1	0	0	0	0	0
9/10/97 HOU	4	1	1	0	0	1	1

9/12/97 @Atl	4	1	1	0	0	0	1
9/13/97 @Atl	4	1	0	0	0	0	0
9/14/97 @Atl	3	0	2	2	0	0	0
9/15/97 @Fla	4	1	2	0	0	1	3
9/16/97 @Fla	2	2	1	0	0	1	1
9/17/97 @SD	4	2	2	0	0	2	4
9/18/97 @SD	4	1	2	0	0	1	3
9/19/97 @LA	4	0	0	0	0	0	0
9/20/97 @LA	3	0	1	1	0	0	1
9/21/97 @LA	4	1	0	0	0	0	0
9/23/97 SF	5	1	2	0	0	0	1
9/24/97 SF	4	1	1	1	0	0	1
9/26/97 LA	3	1	1	0	0	1	1
Totals	568	143	208	46	4	49	130

AVERAGE: .366

Kevin Brown:
That's Kevin with a "K"

Author: Jacqueline Salman
ISBN: 1-58261-050-9

Kevin was born in McIntyre, Georgia and played college baseball for Georgia Tech. Since then he has become one of baseball's most dominant pitchers and when on top of his game, he is virtually unhittable.

Kevin transformed the Florida Marlins and San Diego Padres into World Series contenders in consecutive seasons, and now he takes his winning attitude and talent to the Los Angeles Dodgers.

Larry Walker:
Canadian Rocky

Author: Tony DeMarco
ISBN: 1-58261-052-5

Growing up in Canada, Larry had his sights set on being a hockey player. He was a skater, not a slugger, but when a junior league hockey coach left him off the team in favor of his nephew, it was hockey's loss and baseball's gain.

Although the Rockies' star is known mostly for his hitting, he has won three Gold Glove awards, and has worked hard to turn himself into a complete, all-around ballplayer. Larry became the first Canadian to win the MVP award.

Curt Schilling: Phillie Phire!

Author: Paul Hagen
ISBN: 1-58261-055-x

Born in Anchorage, Alaska, Schilling has found a warm reception from the Philadelphia Phillies faithful. He has amassed 300+ strikeouts in the past two seasons and even holds the National League record for most strikeouts by a right handed pitcher at 319.

This book tells of the difficulties Curt faced being traded several times as a young player, and how he has been able to deal with off-the-field problems.

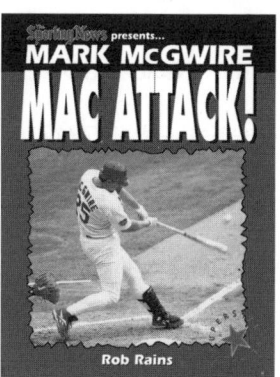

Mark McGwire: Mac Attack!

Author: Rob Rains
ISBN: 1-58261-004-5

Mac Attack! describes how McGwire overcame poor eyesight and various injuries to become one of the most revered hitters in baseball today. He quickly has become a legendary figure in St. Louis, the home to baseball legends such as Stan Musial, Lou Brock, Bob Gibson, Red Schoendienst and Ozzie Smith. McGwire thought about being a police officer growing up, but he hit a home run in his first Little League at-bat and the rest is history.

Roger Clemens: Rocket Man!

Author: Kevin Kernan
ISBN: 1-58261-128-9

Alex Rodriguez: A-plus Shortstop

ISBN: 1-58261-104-1

Baseball
SuperStar Series Titles

Collect Them All!

___ Sandy and Roberto Alomar:
Baseball Brothers

___ Kevin Brown: Kevin with a "K"

___ Roger Clemens: Rocket Man!

___ Juan Gonzalez: Juan Gone!

___ Mark Grace: Winning With Grace

___ Ken Griffey, Jr.: The Home Run Kid

___ Tony Gwynn: Mr. Padre

___ Derek Jeter: The Yankee Kid

___ Randy Johnson: Arizona Heat!

___ Pedro Martinez: Throwing Strikes

___ Mike Piazza: Mike and the Mets

___ Alex Rodriguez: A-plus Shortstop

___ Curt Schilling: Philly Phire!

___ Sammy Sosa: Slammin' Sammy

___ Mo Vaughn: Angel on a Mission

___ Omar Vizquel:
The Man with a Golden Glove

___ Larry Walker: Canadian Rocky

___ Bernie Williams: Quiet Superstar

___ Mark McGwire: Mac Attack!